NATIONAL GALLERY OF IRELAND | GAILEARAÍ NÁISIÚNTA NA hÉIREANN

MASQUERADE & SPECTACLE

THE CIRCUS AND THE TRAVELLING FAIR IN THE WORK OF JACK B. YEATS

Director's Foreword

This exhibition commemorates the 50th anniversary of the death of one of Ireland's most loved painters, Jack B. Yeats. Among the inhabitants of his painted universe certain types stand out, many drawn from the artist's vivid recollections of those periods of his youth spent in rural Ireland. Some became constant motifs in his work throughout his life, working either from recent observation or reflected memory. Many of these subjects had a particular significance for the artist over and above the rudiments of simple portrayal.

A particularly rich vein of inspiration for Yeats was the circus and associated entertainments. Wherever he resided, whether it was London, Dublin or Sligo, Yeats was always drawn to these exotic performances which held such hold on the imagination of the general public who craved an escape from the humdrum existence of their daily lives.

In this exhibition Dr. Róisín Kennedy presents a range of compositions drawn from both the Gallery's own extensive holdings and from public and private collections, to illustrate just how fertile and significant the world of the sawdust ring was for the artist. Whilst noting the personal dimension in such imagery, she also relates his treatment of such subject matter to that of other masters of the modern European tradition.

The exhibition is being mounted in the new home for the Yeats Museum, in a recently refurbished area adjacent to the entrance lobby at the Merrion Square entrance. This space will host the Yeats collection until the permanent home for the museum is delivered as part of the NDP funded Master Development Plan. We are grateful to the Office of Public Works for their management of this project.

The opening of the Yeats Museum in 1999 came about as a result of the extraordinary gift of Anne Yeats and the Yeats family who, through an act of selfless generosity have ensured that much of the artist's private estate is now held in trust for the benefit and enjoyment of the public. The present exhibition builds on this achievement, soliciting the support of private collectors who have made paintings available for show. We are grateful to Pioneer Investments for their generous sponsorship of this exhibition.

Raymond Keaveney
Director
National Gallery of Ireland

Sponsor's Foreword

Pioneer Investments is delighted to support the *Masquerade and Spectacle* exhibition of Jack B. Yeats which illustrates the innovative and creative talents of Yeats in many works that have not been seen before.

As we celebrate the 50th anniversary of the death of Yeats, one of Ireland's favourite sons, we recall Pioneer Investments' own values of tradition and innovation. Our roots go back to 1928 when Yeats would have been in his prime. For almost 80 years we have been a leading innovator in the investment management industry, staying true to our Pioneering methods using a consistent and yet innovative approach to build a world class asset management business.

In Dublin, our European Investment hub, we manage and administer over €120 billion in assets on behalf of third party intermediaries, institutions and high net worth clients from around the world. As the largest front office manager in Ireland, Pioneer Investments employs approximately 20 different nationalities among the 500 staff covering a wide range of functions including Investment Management, Fundamental and Quantitative Research, Corporate functions including Legal, Compliance, Risk, HR, Finance and IT, Middle Office and Marketing.

Having established a presence in Dublin in the mid 90's, we have grown significantly and expect to continue growing and developing our business here, with increased concentration of many global functions in Dublin. We are proud of the talented people we have working in Pioneer Investments, all of whom have been instrumental to our success and who continue to enable us to grow and prosper in Dublin.

We are extremely proud of our association with the arts through our partnership with the National Gallery of Ireland. We hope you will enjoy the exhibition and trust this catalogue will be a lasting memory of *Masquerade and Spectacle*.

Robert Richardson
CEO
Pioneer Investment Management Limited

Acknowledgements

Any serious understanding of Yeats's work rests on the considerable achievements of Dr. Hilary Pyle whose publications on the artist have provided invaluable information and insights into all aspects of his life and work. I would like to thank Dr. Pyle for her encouragement and scholarship.

The National Gallery of Ireland is extremely fortunate in being in possession of the Yeats Archive. This vast array of archival material and artworks, originally belonging to Jack Yeats, was presented by his niece Anne to the gallery in 1996, when Dr. Pyle was Yeats Curator. It has provided me with important contextual material such as the circus ephemera collected by Yeats. In addition it also contains numerous sketchbooks which reveal Yeats's fascination with travelling fairs and circuses. This body of material provides the backbone to the National Gallery's collection of Yeats's paintings, some of which are included in this exhibition. It is also of unique value in understanding Yeats and the contexts in which he worked. I thank the Yeats family for their ongoing support and interest in the Archive and in the Yeats Collection.

I would like to thank the private collectors who have generously lent their paintings. A number of individuals have been helpful in locating works and liaising with owners. In this regard I thank Michelle Archer and Leslie Waddington of Waddington Galleries, Claire Bailey-Coombs and Jonathan Horwich of Christie's, Arabella Bishop and Frances Christie of Sotheby's, Pat Murphy of the OPW Art Management Group, Theo Waddington, John de Vere White, Rory Guthrie, David Britton, and Karen Reihill. Public galleries have also been extremely helpful - Jessica O'Donnell and Liz Forster of the Dublin City Gallery, the Hugh Lane, Emer McGarry of Models Arts and Niland Gallery, Sligo, and Siobhán O'Reilly of Limerick City Gallery of Art.

Within the National Gallery I would like to acknowledge the professionalism and practical advice and support of my colleagues who have all contributed enormously to the success of this exhibition. In particular I thank Fionnuala Croke, Head of Exhibitions, Susan O'Connor, Kim Smit, Felicia Tan, Orla O'Brien, Valerie Keogh and Dr. Marie Bourke. Marie McFeely and Louise Morgan have overseen Rights and Reproductions. Roy Hewson, with the aid of Chris O'Toole, has done a wonderful job with photography. Kevin Kelly and Sheila Dooley, art handlers, installed the exhibition. Conservation was undertaken by Ele Von Monschaw, Michie Konishi, Ranson Davey, Pat McBride and Louise O'Connor. Research and Library Services were extremely helpful, in particular Andrea Lydon, Catherine Sheridan and Victor McGowan. Dr. Brendan Rooney, Niamh MacNally and Donal Maguire provided useful editorial advice. For the production of the catalogue I thank Lydia Furlong, and for superb design work, Jason Ellams. Finally I acknowledge the valuable and insightful contributions made to the catalogue entries by Donal Maguire and Iain Wynn-Jones.

Dr. Róisín Kennedy
Yeats Curator, NGI Fellowship Scholar,
(appointed by the NGI Fellowship Committee).

An Introduction

The Circus

Jack Yeats's interest in the circus coincided with its gradual decline from being a major form of popular entertainment in the late Victorian era to its eclipse by cinema in the mid 20th century. In more recent times the circus has reinvented itself and revived its reputation as a creative art form, a fact of which Yeats might have approved.[1] Yeats, who was always sceptical of the picture house, preferred the spontaneous and unpredictable nature of live theatre and spectacle to the enclosed, anonymous world of celluloid diversion.[2] One of the circus's greatest attractions for Yeats was the dynamic that it created between the performers and their audience. His numerous depictions of the subject highlight this sense of excitement and anticipation. The circus and the side-show also provided Yeats with a rich metaphor for the role of the artist in contemporary society.

The origins of the modern circus can be traced back to the establishment of equestrian displays in London in the 18th century. The most significant of these was Philip Astley's 'Riding School', founded in Lambeth in 1768. Equestrian displays had been a feature of country fairs for centuries but Astley's setting of the event in a circular arena and his forceful marketing of the performances were key developments in the creation of the modern circus. By the early 19th century permanent circuses, centring on equestrian acts, were established in London and were also appearing in Paris, St. Petersburg and the United States. Astley began making yearly visits to Dublin in 1773 as part of his expansion of the circus into the provinces. He subsequently built a permanent amphitheatre in Peter Street in the south of the city.[3]

Fig. 1: Jack B. Yeats, *View of Circus at Dartmouth*, Sketchbook x164, Strete Circus 1898, Yeats Archive, NGI.

Out of these permanent city based venues, the travelling circus developed during the course of the 19th century. Its appearance was partly a response to the strict laws governing the management of theatres in this period, and its prioritisation of unscripted acts was another strategy used by its proprietors to bypass such restrictions. American circuses played an enormous role in the creation of the archetypal Big Top circus as it was in the United States that the use of tents rather than permanent buildings became the norm. Brightly painted circus wagons were also a feature of American circuses, with larger companies owning their own trains to transport big numbers of staff and animals across the continent. Famous American circuses such as Barnum and Bailey's *Greatest Show on Earth* toured Europe in the 1880s and 1890s. Jack Yeats attended and sketched one of their performances at Dartmouth in 1899. His sketchbook records such sights as a Tattooed Lady, a Giant, a Japanese rope artiste and the vending of 'American Popcorn', a rare commodity in England at that time.[4]

Modern literature and cinema has often represented the circus as a site of degenerate behaviour. In fact circuses were, in many ways, models of Victorian respectability and conformity. Most were family establishments and they stressed their connection to royal or official sponsorship in their programmes and often in their names. They followed the conventions of contemporary business etiquette with seating and ticketing arrangements based on a tiered system, with the most expensive seats commanding the best views of the performance.[5]

Circuses tended to follow an established programme which was familiar to the audience. A typical performance began with a procession of circus performers and animals, followed by equestrian acts, acrobats and trapeze artistes. These specialised feats were interspersed by clown acts which often imitated or even partook in the former, upending the seriousness of the event. Leading equestrians, acrobats and clowns became well-known celebrities and their names were prominently displayed in the gaudy advertisements produced as part of the elaborate publicity for the circus. In addition to the central tent, circuses were also marked by side-shows with carnival acts and menageries of wild animals and displays of human oddities.

These sideshows and menageries as well as the travelling circus's ability to perform in remote locations, far from the conventional metropolitan centres of popular entertainment, meant that it attracted a diverse audience from all social backgrounds. This populist aspect was of great interest to Yeats, many of whose paintings and drawings are concerned with the effect of the circus in a rural, rather than an urban context. Yeats admired the opinion of the ordinary spectator, rejecting any hierarchical view of art as an elitist occupation.

Fig. 2: Jack B. Yeats, *View of Circus Ring and Audience*, Sketchbook 168, Greystones Martin Harvey, 1912, Yeats Archive, NGI.

This anti-intellectual stance extended to his own work. As he wrote to his American patron, John Quinn: '.... an Irish peasant is a better judge of art than a Whistler or a Corot.'[6]

Small scale travelling circuses provided a focus of great excitement and escape in the immediate locality. Their performances always contained some unpredictable moments due to simple factors such as the weather, the attitude of the crowd, and not least, the real risk of a performer injuring him or herself. These elements made each performance a unique event subject to chance and incident and quite unlike more conventional forms of public entertainment.

Fig. 3: Jack B. Yeats, *The Circus*, Illustration to John M. Synge, *In Wicklow, West Kerry and Connemara*, 1911, facing p.76.

John Millington Synge's description of a travelling circus in Dingle in the early 1900s encapsulates the divergent response generated by the event. Fearful that the tent might collapse at any moment, the performers had to contend with soggy conditions and a drunken, rowdy audience. Like Yeats, Synge's interest was aroused as much by the relationship of the crowd to the circus people, as by the performance itself:

> 'At the entrance a rather riotous crowd began to surge in so quickly that there was some danger of the place being rushed. Word was sent across the ring, and in a moment three or four of the women performers, with long streaming ulsters buttoned over their thighs, ran out from behind the scenes and threw themselves into the crowd, forcing back the wild hillside people, fishwomen and drunken sailors, in an extraordinary tumult of swearing, wrestling and laughter. These women seemed to enjoy this part of their work, and shrieked with amusement when two or three of them fell on some enormous farmer or publican and nearly dragged him to the ground. Here and there among the people I could see a little party of squireens and their daughters, in the fashions of five years ago, trying, not always successfully, to reach the shilling seats. The crowd was now so thick I could see little more than the heads of the performers, who had at last come into the ring, and many of the shorter women who were near me must have seen nothing the whole evening, yet they showed no sign of impatience., ...'.

John Millington Synge[7]

The Circus in Modern Art

The circus was an established theme in avant-garde European art by the time Jack Yeats became interested in it as a subject for his own work. It was part of a much broader area of subject matter, connected to the world of cabaret and café concerts. For the French Impressionists and Post-Impressionists the circus provided a modern urban theme closely connected to the new recreational facilities which were opening up in Paris and other European cities. This modern commodification of leisure was central to the circus with its emphasis on advertising and ritual. Artists such as Edouard Manet and Georges Seurat explored this aspect of the subject in very different ways. But they were primarily interested in the permanent circuses created in municipal centres whereas Yeats was drawn to the travelling circus and its impact on the immediate rural population.

Fig. 4: Edgar Degas, *Miss La La at the Cirque Fernando*, 1879, National Gallery, London.

The conflicting vistas of performers and audience to be found in the circus echoed the new perspectives created by photography and the Western discovery of Japanese woodblock prints in the mid to late 19th century. This new visualisation is evident in Yeats's exploitation of the cut-off composition and was a feature of the work of Henri de Toulouse-Lautrec and Edgar Degas. In addition, the physical arrangement of the circus ring and tent provided modernist artists with the opportunity of using oblique perspectives and unusual viewpoints to evoke a contemporary experience of spectatorship. Audiences at the circus or sideshow had to contend with the distraction of the crowd and outside noises as well as the tent's structure and the constantly changing position of the performers from clowns on ground level to trapeze artists dangling from the ceiling.

This new way of representing the modern spectacle can be seen in Yeats's circus and fair scenes. In such paintings as *The Barrel Man* (cat. 6), the *Circus Dwarf* (cat. 8), and the *Double Jockey Act* (cat. 10), the artist uses a limited palette of strong colours and contrasts diagonal, vertical and horizontal lines to evoke very different moods. One moves from elation in the *Barrel Man* to contemplation in the *Circus Dwarf* to a powerful mixture of exhilaration and tension in the *Double Jockey Act*. In the latter work the combination of strong diagonals in the depiction of the performers and the horizontal forms of the onlookers and the striped decor express, in visual terms, the conflicting emotions and sensations generated by the circus performance.

Yeats was familiar with the work of Degas from exhibitions he attended in London. His influence is evident in many of the watercolours produced by the Irish artist at the turn of the century. Yeats was also aware of Post-Impressionism through his knowledge of the work of the English artist, Walter Sickert. Sickert had worked with Henry MacNeill Whistler and with Degas in Paris in the 1880s. He was one of the foremost advocates of Post-Impressionist art in London when Yeats was beginning his career as a fine artist.[8] In addition Yeats learnt about Post-Impressionist composition and colour through his work as an illustrator and poster designer in England in the 1890s. Such popular manifestations of avant-garde aesthetics were crucially important to Yeats, who drew on a wide range of sources for his work, most of it from the realms of popular culture rather than fine art.

The presence of different races such as Indians, Native Americans and Arabs made the circus a site for the exotic. Its recreation of historical events and imagined scenarios created a suspension of real time and provided an escape from the mundane realities of life outside the tent. This sensation was immediately contradicted by the experience of the circus itself. Its fast moving programme relied on modern technology such as gas or electric lighting for its success. The strange dichotomy which the circus created between real and imagined time, and a modern Western world and a fantasy arena for the bizarre and unusual made it a powerful metaphor for artists who wished to challenge the limits of contemporary expectations.

The circus performer, who had rejected conventional ways of making a living, was of enormous significance to the modern artist. His work and life, like that of the artist, were interconnected and did not follow the domestic professional boundaries established by modern capitalism. The clown, in particular, who was related to the Pierrot and Harlequin figures of earlier centuries, had been established in Western art in the 18th century as a metaphor for the artist and for creativity in general. His outward jovial demeanour and comical performance was seen to mask an inner isolation and suffering. The subject was taken up in the 20th century by artists such as Pablo Picasso and Georges Rouault who emphasised the performer's position as an outsider from society. In Picasso's Rose period the acrobat takes on a clear autobiographical meaning but the subject is also invested with the gravitas of classical art, which lends it a timeless dimension.

Fig. 5: Jack B. Yeats, *Arab on a Camel's Back*, Sketchbook x167, Strete Circus 1898, Yeats Archive, NGI.

Picasso's interpretation of the circus player as symbolic of the artist at odds with modern society is perceptible in Yeats's later paintings of clowns and circus scenes. The clown held a special allure for Yeats who had a lifelong preoccupation with Johnny Patterson, the Singing Clown, who died tragically in 1889. Yeats made his first drawing of Patterson the following year and he continued to appear in his paintings fifty years later. Patterson epitomised the success of the circus performer who, coming from humble origins, achieved great wealth and fame. But his chosen occupation contributed to a difficult and complicated personal life and to his untimely death. He died violently as a result of injuries received at the hands of a crowd who did not share the political sentiments of one of his songs, (see cat. 12).

Yeats was intrigued by the ability of the clown to hold his audience's attention through comedy and song. His dominance of the strange world of the circus is a central theme in many of Yeats's circus paintings, such as *The Singing Clown* (cat. 12) and *They Love Me* (cat. 20). In *This Grand Conversation was Under the Rose* (cat. 14), the figure of the clown is depicted off-duty, seated backstage with a rather formidable female haute école rider. This bizarre scene refuses to offer the viewer any simplistic meaning although the figure of the clown has been construed as autobiographical. It seems clear that Yeats, like other modern artists, equated the circus performer with himself as artist. While both could wield tremendous power while creating art, both were also misunderstood and misrepresented by society at large.

Yeats's engagement with the circus and travelling fair was related to the mainstream European interest in the subject in his own day. In 1936 two of his paintings were included in an exhibition on the theme of the circus at the Leger Galleries in London.[9] Among the 49 other artists in the show were Picasso and Rouault. Like them Yeats was aware of the hierarchy that existed within the circus itself and it prompted his choice of subject. He was drawn to the underdog - the barrel man, the dwarf and the clown - to their role in the creation and maintenance of the spectacle. It was their privilege and their burden to enact the kind of physical and emotional extremes from which the rest of humanity is normally excluded.

Fig. 6: Pablo Picasso, *Two Acrobats with a Dog*, 1905, Museum of Modern Art, New York.

Yeats and the Circus

Yeats's long fascination with the circus began with childhood visits to fairs and small travelling circuses in Sligo, where he was brought up by his grandparents. When, in 1887, at the age of sixteen, he joined his parents in London, he became a frequent visitor to the spectacular London circuses and related establishments. The Yeats family lived in Earl's Court, close to the location of Buffalo Bill's *Great Realistic Exhibition of Western Novelties*, which was brought over from the United States as part of the Golden Jubilee celebrations of Queen Victoria's reign in 1887. Buffalo Bill, or Colonel William Cody, was a real life cowboy hero who had hunted and herded his way across the American plains, often coming under attack from Red Indians. Buffalo Bill's recreation of the Wild West was not strictly speaking a circus, but its use of sharp shooting, knife throwing and lasso spinning was very influential on contemporary circus acts.[10] His show featured Annie Oakley, the original Deadwood Coach, and a huge cast of genuine cowboys, cowgirls and Red Indians. The latter, who performed daring horseback acts, made a distinct impression on Yeats and recur in a number of his watercolours and later oil paintings. His admiration for their horsemanship and courage, as seen at Col. Cody's *Wild West Show*, also contributed to Yeats's romantic depictions of jockeys and horsemen in the west of Ireland.

Fig. 7: Cover of *Buffalo Bill's Wild West Historical Scenes*, 1892, Yeats Archive, NGI.

The sketchbooks, which Yeats began to use in the mid 1890s, show that the artist frequently attended the circus at the end of that decade. He was living in Devon and working as an illustrator for a wide range of London periodicals, contributing humorous cartoons and drawings of sporting events. At the same period Yeats was beginning to produce the dramatic and colourful watercolour paintings with which he established his reputation as a fine artist in the early 20th century. Between March 1897 and June 1899 he attended and sketched, often in detail, five circuses in the west of England and one at Gort in Co. Galway. These sketches formed the nucleus of the numerous watercolours and illustrations of circuses produced by the artist in the following years. Indeed he returned to many of their themes and motifs in his oil paintings of later decades.

Some of the circuses that Yeats attended were amongst the most famous of their day. Four Pawrs Circus, which Jack sketched at Dartmouth in May 1898, featured performing elephants, a hypnotist, numerous clowns and a sensational staircase performance by the Zaccara Troupe of female artistes. Yeats noted in his sketchbook that he had already seen Captain Rowland and his performing elephants at another show at Chertsey in Devon. He annotated his drawings with details of the acts, often noting down the clown's jokes, perhaps thinking of his own work as a cartoonist. Many of the sketches focus on the interface between the local population and the strange phenomenon of the circus with its wild animals, outrageous costumes and its reliance on mechanics and technology. Yeats paid great attention to the programme of circuses which he attended, often pasting folded newspaper advertisements or posters into his pocket-sized sketchbooks.

Yeats sketched Lord John Sanger and Sons' show at Strete in July 1898. Sanger was part of a legendary British circus family, who had adopted the aristocratic title 'Lord' to give their business a regal aura. Lord George, brother of John, was married to a famous female lion tamer, Ellen Chapman, apparently the first woman to put her head in a lion's mouth.[11] Lord John's circus included numerous horses, elephants, man-eating wolves, an untameable lion, camels as well as such exotic performers as the Arabian charioteers and a lady ringmaster.

While many of his watercolours and drawings of these years relate to circuses visited in England, Yeats was beginning to explore the relationship of the travelling circus to rural Ireland in particular. From 1898 he was becoming more focused on Irish subject matter and in 1899 began staging annual one-man shows in Dublin, under the title *Sketches of Life in the West of Ireland*. His sketchbooks reveal his growing interest in local fairs which he visited on his summer journeys around the west of Ireland. The sideshows and entertainments which formed part of these events are similar to those found at the circus. They recur along with circus scenes in Yeats's *A Broadside*, (1908-15) and in his book, *Life in the West of Ireland*, (1912) in which, along with race meetings and horse fairs, the travelling fair and circus are shown to be a central feature of Irish rural life.

When Yeats returned to live in Ireland permanently in 1910 his sketching of circuses was revived. He made several drawings of circuses at Greystones, where he lived, between 1910 and 1914. Many of these depictions of, by now, familiar clowns and equestrian displays are found in sketchbooks which also contain scenes of political tension. The latter include drawings of the search for guns off the Dublin coast, commemorating the shooting of bystanders at Bachelor's Walk and the funeral of O'Donovan Rossa. This mixture of imagery highlights Yeats's ability to

Fig. 8: Poster for John Sanger's Circus, pasted into Sketchbook X167, Strete Circus, 1898, Yeats Archive, NGI.

record and to be aware of the great diversity of human activity.

During this same period the artist was beginning to use memory actively in the creation of his artwork. In a sketchbook of 1915 a view of a circus ring and audience is derived from his memory of a visit to a circus at Greystones on a previous occasion. Many of Yeats's later evocations of the circus and travelling fair in his oil paintings are similarly gleaned from recollections of earlier visits made as a comparatively young man. His 1912 painting of *The Barrel Man* (cat. 6), recalls an earlier visit to a Co. Galway fair when Yeats first sketched this bizarre sideshow feat. In a much later painting, *Humanities Alibi* (1947, Bristol City Museum and Art Gallery), Yeats returns to the same theme, showing a man in a barrel fending off the heavy sticks thrown at him by an excited crowd.[12] In this version, a lower viewpoint is taken so that one can see the top of the barrel and the struggling figure of the man fending off what has now become a never-ending bombardment of missiles. Made towards the end of Yeats's life, the painting resonates with a profound sense of life's ongoing struggle. The earlier heroism and humour of the *Barrel Man* has now been transformed into an existential labour, expressed through the metaphor of a fairground entertainment.

Yeats had produced a large number of watercolours depicting the circus in the period 1897 to 1910, and when he began painting in oils around 1909 the theme continued to be a dominant one. In 1912 he painted three of his most accomplished early oil paintings on the theme - *The Barrel Man*, *The Maggie Man* (cat. 7), and *The Circus Dwarf* (cat. 8). Their sources are a mixture of the distinctively Irish country fair and the more universally understood circus scene of the dwarf in costume. Together they highlight the common theme of humanity as a source of spectacle for his fellow creatures, an idea at the heart of the circus and sideshow experience. Yeats, who was used to covering sporting and theatrical events as a contributor to periodicals, was very familiar with this phenomenon.

Fig. 9: Jack B. Yeats, *Circus, Greystones, Notes from Memory*, Sketchbook 116, Arklow, Greystones, Circus, Schull, 1915, Yeats Archive, NGI.

Between 1916 and 1936 Yeats went on to depict various aspects of the circus performance in numerous oil paintings. Equestrian acts, trapeze artistes and clowns were each afforded special attention. Many of these are drawn together in *They Come They Come* (cat. 13), an exhilarating and colourful depiction of circus performers coming into the ring. In the same years Yeats abandoned his earlier preference for portrait-formatted compositions and began to paint predominantly in landscape format, which allowed him to convey the expanse and diverse spatial levels of the circus. This preference for the wider shape extended to other areas of subject matter, which like the circus paintings, increasingly play on the ambiguous nature of reality and make believe. *Chair-o-Planes* (cat. 11), a fairground scene, is a good example of this ambiguity. Here the device of an airborne merry-go-round upends conventional compositions by placing the active elements, the laughing adults, in the air where they take on the appearance of acrobats or the sort of lavish ceiling decorations found in 19th century theatres and music-halls.

Yeats continued to make occasional sketches of circuses throughout his life and to keep relevant newspaper cuttings. His development as a playwright in the 1920s and 1930s contributed to his interest in the theatrical aspects of the phenomenon. In his play *Apparitions*, published in 1933, Yeats gave instructions that the audience was to be seated around the performance, as in a circus.[13]

In subsequent years Yeats moved away from depictions of specific performances within the circus arena to scenes which reveal the private moments of the performers or to those that expose the relationship of the circus to its wider social and physical environment. Circus artistes are shown resting between acts or moving from the limits of the circus ring into intermediary or more expansive positions, as in *The Cavalier's Farewell to his Steed* (cat. 19), or *This Grand Conversation was Under the Rose* (cat. 14). Such works allow for a closer consideration of the role of the performer rather than the performance itself.

In other later works the transitory nature of the circus and the lives of its performers take precedence. In *Let'em go and take care of Yourselves* (cat. 17), the circus procession races out of the tent into an untamed landscape. In the *Last Dawn but One* (cat. 18), the circus performers begin the arduous task of dismantling their camp and moving on to the next setting. This act is a powerful metaphor for the artist who, when faced with a blank canvas, must create something out of nothing. Such works relate closely to Yeats's paintings of travelling players and vagabonds, represented in this exhibition by *The Entertainers* (cat. 16).

Some of the later circus paintings have been connected directly to events in Yeats's personal life, such as the death of his wife, Cottie, in 1947. This personal loss is believed to have prompted the circus painting, *The Great Tent has Collapsed* (1947, Private Collection). Although begun several months before his wife's death, the work has been widely interpreted in terms of Jack's grieving. In the painting a crowd scurries away while the ringmaster and a bystander look on at a collapsed circus tent which lies blowing in the breeze. Its circus flag is still flying high. As in

Fig. 10: Jack B. Yeats, *'Oh Lord don't be fretting, give him a heavy stick'*, Sketchbook 31, Coole, 1903, Yeats Archive, NGI.

Let 'em Go and Take Care of Yourselves, the circus is related in Yeats's work to the basic human need to survive through the establishment and maintenance of an inner imaginative world which exists apart from immediate physical or emotional needs.

Closely related to this metaphor is the tiny oil painting, *An Embryo of the Circus* (1940, Private Collection), which Yeats claimed recalled a childhood visit to the circus in Sligo. It shows a small child standing in an empty circus ring with the familiar paraphernalia of seating, tent poles and entrance curtain behind him. His confident pose, feet apart, and his alert expression indicate that this is a consummate performer in the making. It is significant that Yeats had an ink sketch of the painting in his studio at the end of his life. Like the child born to the circus, Yeats felt that he was born to be an artist. Asked why he had become a painter, he declared 'because I was the son of a painter'.[14] His statement acknowledges the complex familial, social and economic ties that apply as much to the artist and the circus performer as to any other profession. But it also suggests that Yeats was nurtured in a milieu where creativity and imagination were given particular emphasis.

The development of Yeats's art, from sharply observed realism to his later expressionist paintings, bear witness to the breath of his imagination. The work shows a constant drive to experiment and to push the boundaries of the craft of painting. In Yeats's later oil paintings areas of deep impasto are juxtaposed with sections which are barely covered in thin washes of colour, if at all. The paint is applied in loose strokes with a palette knife or directly from the tube. The result can be both exhilarating and confusing. It forces the viewer to engage with the painting, to look at it carefully in order to decipher the forms within it. By working in this manner, Yeats draws attention to the physical nature of painting and by extension to its construction.

Fig. 11: Jack B. Yeats, Pen sketch of *An Embryo of the Circus*, c.1943, Yeats Archive, NGI.

Yeats's choice of subject matter, particularly the masquerade and spectacle of the circus, is intrinsically connected to the manner in which he painted. Both are concerned with the creation of a world of fantasy and illusion. In both the physical formation of this world is an inherent part of its meaning. Like a circus performer Yeats was not afraid of taking risks. His later paintings frequently appear to defy the laws of physics. Like his earlier psychologically charged images, they draw the viewer into Yeats's particular version of the spectacular.

Dr. Róisín Kennedy, Yeats Curator

1 In April 2007 the Arts Council of Ireland advertised for a Head of Theatre and Circus, thus acknowledging the central position of the circus to Irish cultural life.
2 Purser 1991, pp.37-40.
3 Speaight 1980, pp.41-42.
4 Sketchbook 171, *Circus, Paris, Strete, Barnums*, 1899, Yeats Archive, NGI.
5 Stoddart 2000.
6 Letter of John Quinn to AE, 2 May 1904, quoted in Potterton 1993, p.110.
7 Synge 1911, pp.76-77.
8 The two men became friends after Yeats left England in 1910. See Pyle 1970, pp.108-09.
9 *The Circus,* Leger Galleries, London, 8 December 1936 to 16 January 1937. Yeats exhibited two paintings, *Johnny Patterson Singing 'Bridget Donohue'* and *The Double Jockey Act*.
10 Speaight 1980, p.150.
11 *ibid*, p.83.
12 *Humanities Alibi* is reproduced in Snoddy 1991, plate 18.
13 Purser 1991, p.31.
14 Pyle 1970, p.11.

1

Fortune and Her Wheel, 1902

Pencil and poster paint on card, 28.54 x 43.5 cm
Courtesy of Sligo Municipal Collection & Model Arts and Niland Gallery

Chaucer, Dante, Machiavelli and Shakespeare have all written on the concept of Fortune and her wheel, but here Yeats brings the subject down to earth with a witty image of a fortune teller easily parting the gullible from their money. A crowd forms around her, faces looking up with awe, anger and bemusement. One character walks towards us chewing his knuckles with worry after paying his money and getting news that we can only guess is bad.

Fortune and Her Wheel is a great example of Yeats's ability to inject drama into his recordings and sketches of Irish life and the Irish people. He presents the Irish peasant as naturally exuberant, and emphasises their quirkiness and diversity of character.

This watercolour was one of the first Yeats works owned by John Quinn the Irish American lawyer and patron to the Yeats family. Originally patron to John Butler Yeats (Jack's father), Quinn was instrumental in helping W. B. Yeats in America, and was a strong admirer and supporter of Jack Yeats's painting. The two men corresponded over the course of twenty-three years and their letters reveal much about Yeats's development as an artist in this period.[1]

I. W-J.

1 Potterton 1993.

JACK B YEATS

2

Crystal Palace, c.1903

Pencil, watercolour and gouache on paper, 18 x 26 cm
Private Collection

This early watercolour recalls a visit made by Yeats to a Wild West show at the Crystal Palace, London in 1892. Similar to the extravaganzas put on by Buffalo Bill in Earl's Court, this entertainment centred on the daring deeds of the Red Indian or Native American. The figure is dressed in a red and green costume with an elaborate headdress. His face is brightly painted in the same colours and he swings a tomahawk in the air above his head. The Indian appears to be travelling on horseback but, on closer inspection, his roller skates are clearly visible beneath the hobby-horse prop which covers the lower half of his body. He is, in fact, skating at great speed across the wooden floor of the gigantic Crystal Palace. Another Indian on a hobby-horse can be seen in the far distance to the left.

Yeats has sketched out the interior of the Palace in some detail using the straight lines of the floorboards to guide the perspective. The diagonal slant of these lines adds to the sense of movement in the painting. On top of the pencil Yeats uses blue-violet over paint and very strong greens and reds in the details of the Red Indian and his horse. This use of vibrant colour is typical of Yeats's watercolours of this period which owe a debt to Post-Impressionism in their deployment of the abstract decorative qualities of pure colour and geometric form.

The subject of Red Indians skating on hobby-horses recurs in a number of later works by Yeats, such as *The Red Man of the Rink* (1950, Private Collection). An image of Red Indians waiting behind the stage curtain at the Crystal Palace featured in *A Broadside*, March 1911. The hobby-horse with its distinctive and rather childlike polka dot coat is also found in *The Cavalier's Farewell to His Steed* (cat. 19). The figure of the Red Indian with his bizarre appearance and physical prowess appealed greatly to Yeats's imagination. However the subject was always represented by Yeats in terms of the circus or theatrical performance. His depiction of the Red Indian highlighted the construction of him as a figure of entertainment, who belonged in the realms of fantasy rather than reality.

R.K.

JACK B. YEATS

3

A Travelling Circus, 1906

Watercolour on paper, 26 x 35.5 cm
Dublin City Gallery, The Hugh Lane

In this watercolour, brimming with life and excitement, the business of circus preparations continues on whilst the crowds arrive at the Big Top. A large stream of townsfolk effectively leads the viewer's eye towards the rear of the image and to the circus tent. Close to the entrance is a caravan, the side of which advertises the kinds of unusual animals and reptiles that are to be seen. In the centre of the composition, close to the crowd, stands the circus ringmaster, wearing a red jacket and black top hat. He creates a path through the people so as to let the circus hands bring across the horses.

This image sees Yeats in observer role once again, possibly amalgamating several separate observations together to form this image. Barefoot boys sit on the front wall where they can get a good view of the hustle and bustle. At the back of the tent a small group of townsfolk have an impromptu meeting with some of the performers. All the while the business of the travelling circus continues in all corners of the painting.

Altogether this busy, noisy image contrasts strongly with the quiet and sparseness of *An Occupation* (cat. 5).

I. W-J.

ZOO ANIMALS AND
REPTILES

4

The Circus Chariot, 1910

Watercolour and crayon on paper, 25.4 x 35.5 cm
NGI 6361

A man dressed as an ancient Briton or Celt drives his chariot and three horses hard through pelting rain. This scene is drawn from a memory of a similar indoor performance seen in England.[1] Yeats has transplanted the action to Ireland and to the outdoors where we can see the circus tent in the background. The colours are deep and solemn, browns and lilacs predominate, only lifted by the bright red of the harness and the shield. Yeats's technical skill is evident in the depiction of the torrential rain. Through the combination of watercolour and crayon he gives this image drama and dynamism.

This chariot act made a strong impression on Yeats and it recurred in a number of other works. In *A Broadside,* September 1908, Yeats included an ink and watercolour illustration called *The Charioteer.* In this image the charioteer is depicted in detail from behind as he passes through a town as part of the circus procession. He wears a plume of horsehair on his helmet, and a long cloak. The figure, and the chariot that he is driving, resemble those found in this painting although they are depicted in a very different manner.

I. W-J.

1 Pyle 1993, p.166.

5

An Occupation, 1910

Oil on canvas, 28 x 38 cm
Private Collection, Ireland

In a moment of relative quiet, away from the main tent of the circus, an old man crosses the field towards a wheeled cage. In the cage is a bear, his nose poking out from the bars, sniffing the air and sensing the approaching man who is struggling with a bucket of meat. It is not clear whether this is an incident during the setting up of the circus or a moment when the circus comes down and moves to its next location. Yeats is very much in documentary mode in the creation of this image, sketching behind-the-scenes life in the travelling fair. He concentrates on the mundane side of circus life, in contrast to the energy and noise of the public areas.

The circus and fair held a special attraction for Yeats, as they were one of the high points of his youth in Sligo. Many of his paintings and watercolours focus on the sensational aspects of the shows - the procession, the acrobats, clowns and performers. But this painting shows that he was as interested in the human element and the work that went on backstage. Yeats gave the work a warm witty title, highlighting the humorous aspect of the scene.

I. W-J.

JACK B. YEATS

6

The Barrel Man, 1912

Oil on panel, 35.5 x 23 cm
Private Collection

Painted from a low viewpoint and framed against an expanse of pink and blue sky, the Barrel Man defends himself against the barrage of sticks being flung at him from a crowd beyond the composition to the left. As a sideshow at fairs and strand races, one could pay a penny for a few sticks to try and hit the Barrel Man whilst he, goading and laughing, ducks into the barrel or deflects the bombardment with the baton in his hand.

From the warm colours of pink, orange and ochre as well as the strong modelling of light and shade, we can assume that it is a late summer afternoon. The viewpoint is focused on the figure of the Barrel Man. We are not shown the rest of the fair or the strand races. Instead Yeats concentrates on the energy of the moment as conveyed by the Barrel Man's facial expression and his wide-open eyes.

Yeats returned to the theme of the Barrel Man several times in his early drawings and watercolours. These draw on observations made at a fair in Gort, Co. Galway that he sketched in 1903.[1] He used the subject most strikingly in a later allegorical oil painting, *Humanities Alibi* (1947, City of Bristol Museum and Art Gallery). *The Barrel Man* was exhibited at the famous Armory Show in the United States in 1913 (see cat. 8).

I. W-J.

1 Recorded in Sketchbook 31, *Coole*, 1903, Yeats Archive, NGI. See p.21.

7

The Maggie Man, 1912

Oil on panel, 35.5 x 23 cm
Dublin City Gallery, The Hugh Lane

With its matching dimensions and similar fairground subject, *The Maggie Man* complements *The Barrel Man* (cat. 6). This time the target of the batons is the Maggie, a word derived from the Irish 'gleas magaidh' or 'object of ridicule'.[1] The barefooted Maggie Man collects the thrown batons to return to the next customer. The strong red of the Maggie itself and the Maggie Man's waistcoat stand out against the canvas material of the shy, creating a visual connection between the worker and his sideshow.

Is the Maggie Man nervous of the approaching background figure? Is that burly figure the proprietor of the fair; his name written on the banner that we see at the top of the frame? The expression on the Maggie Man's face hints at an underlying tension thus giving the image an entertaining psychological dimension. The Maggie Man appears to be as much a victim as the Maggie itself.

The subject was treated in a similarly witty way in 'Maggie' reproduced in *Life in the West of Ireland* (1912).[2] This time the Maggie Man is not only at risk from the flying batons of the customers but also from a formidable female figure, presumably his wife. She wields a baton above his head.

I. W-J.

1 Pyle 1992, I, p.34
2 Yeats 1912, p.19.

J McGOWAN
JACK B. YEATS

8

The Circus Dwarf, 1912

Oil on canvas, 91.5 x 61 cm
Private Collection, Ireland

The Circus Dwarf was rejected by the RHA when Yeats submitted it to its annual exhibition in 1912, but was included in the Armory Show, one of the most famous exhibitions of the early 20th century, held in New York and Chicago in 1913. It was one of six works by Yeats to be shown in this major exhibition of European modernist art, where it hung alongside work by Picasso, Matisse, Duchamp and other avant-garde artists. (See cat. 6).

The figure of a dwarf is shown standing in a corner of a circus tent surrounded by various props including a large rose encrusted hoop through which a horse or an acrobat might jump. He is leaning on a trestle seat, with his hand tightly clenched. Yeats avoids caricaturing the figure and presents the sitter as a self-possessed individual who is keeping a watchful eye on the proceedings. Warm reds and browns dominate the palette of the painting and connect the dwarf to his surroundings. But they also contribute to the claustrophobic aura of the scene. The colours are relieved only by the glimpses of white sky visible through the openings in the tent's roof, which reflect a patch of white light back onto the dwarf's forehead.

The composition of the painting is made up of a series of vertical forms, relieved by diagonal lines. Yeats repeats these competing vertical and diagonal patterns throughout the work. This carefully controlled composition augments the intense mood of the painting. The use of diagonals and verticals can be contrasted with that found in the *Double Jockey Act* (cat. 10), where they are used to impart a feeling of movement and excitement.

R.K.

9

The Circus Wagon, 1912

Oil on canvas, 61 x 91.5 cm
Private Collection

Under a black and ominous night sky, a horse drawn circus arrives at a town. The church and its moonlit steeple dominate the skyline. There are no crowds of people welcoming the arrivals, no sense of excitement at the festivities to come. Instead the orange wagon and the team of horses seem to steal into the town under cover of darkness. Much attention is given to the intense dark sky and the dramatic highlights on the piebald horses. This theatrical use of lighting has been compared to that found in the work of Goya.[1]

Yeats used the motif of the circus procession many times. One of the most notable is *The Circus Procession in the Town,* an illustration for his book, *Life in the West of Ireland* (1912).[2] Here a horse drawn caravan parades through a narrow street, the proportions of the carriage exaggerated to almost the height of the buildings. On either side of the carriage sit performers wearing enormous masks and waving at the townsfolk.

The Circus Wagon is probably the best known of Yeats's circus processions. Bruce Arnold has identified in it the artist's tentative move towards oil paint. The use of a horizontal landscape-format adds to the strong sense of movement evoked by the long line of horses.[3]

I. W-J.

1 Pyle 1992, 1, p.37.
2 Yeats 1912, p.73.
3 Arnold 1998, p.180.

10

Double Jockey Act, 1916

Oil on canvas, 61 x 46 cm
NGI 1737

Equestrian acts have always been a significant feature of the circus programme. Here Yeats depicts a performance known as the double jockey act in which two jockeys balance on the rump of a horse as it canters swiftly around the circus ring. The jockey's balancing act was aided by dusting the animals back with powdered resin; consequently the horses became known as 'rosinbacks'.[1] Yeats may have seen such an act being performed in the ring of a travelling circus in Sligo and based this painting on the many sketches he produced while travelling throughout the county.

A clown gallops enthusiastically alongside the horse imitating both the movement of the animal and the jockeys who wave their hats in the air at the pinnacle of their act. The night-time performance is lit by the dim gas flares, positioned on the central post, that pick out essential details but leave the audience shrouded in darkness.

The painting is a fine example of Yeats's growing confidence in the use of oil paint. It displays his almost complete abandonment of the strong line and graphic style that exemplified his earlier work for a technique characterised by areas of thick impasto and broad brush work. Yeats's appreciation of pattern is also evident in the contrasting horizontal and diagonal shapes and thick dabs of colour applied in a select palette of blue, red and white.

Many artists have celebrated the skill and aesthetics of equestrian acts in painting and Yeats's work bears resemblance to Georges Seurat's *Le Cirque* (1891). Although the grand arena and bourgeois entertainment depicted in Seurat's work is far from the world of Yeats's humble circus tent, there is an uncanny similarity in the composition and content of both paintings.

D.M.

1 Croft-Cooke & Cotes 1976, p.125.

JACK B YEATS

11

Chair-O-Planes, 1926

Oil on canvas, 46 x 61 cm
Permanent Collection of Limerick City Gallery of Art

Yeats captures the colour and thrill of a familiar fairground ride. Chair-o-planes, a variation of the carousal, consists of simple seats suspended on chains attached to a rotating top. The centrifugal force that it produced causes the seats to be thrown outwards. It was a regular attraction at carnivals and seaside fairs and Yeats's picture is derived directly from a sketch that he made at a Dublin fair-ground in 1925.[1]

A good example of Yeats's working method of the period, the painting reveals the intrinsic role of his sketchbooks. During the 1920s he began to draw more regularly upon imagery from his sketches as inspiration for the subjects of his oil paintings. The original sketch for *Chair-o-planes* is a vague rendering of the ride, concerned with the arrangement of composition over detail. The apparent haste and vigour with which it was executed is appropriate to the liveliness of the subject. By applying paint in fluid unrestrained brushstrokes this effect is replicated in the final oil.

The application of pigment in the work is illustrative of Yeats's increasing confidence in the expressive use of colour. The structure of the ride is a shimmering kaleidoscope set against a deep-blue evening sky under which a throng of people are rendered in an assortment of reds and browns. Amidst the explosion of pigment a leg swings freely from one of the chairs and the face of a man and a girl are picked out. The girl smiles gleefully and the man glances at another woman as they spin and race by the viewer. Their fleeting expressions convey both the excitement of the moment and Yeats's fondness for the simple aspects of human life.

D.M.

1 Sketchbook 211, *Dublin, Burren, Coole, Valencia, Darrynane*, 1925, Yeats Archive, NGI. The subsequent sketch in the book is of a carousel.

JACK B YEATS

12

The Singing Clown, 1928

Oil on canvas, 46 x 61 cm
Courtesy of Sligo Municipal Collection & Model Arts and Niland Gallery

At a basic level this painting is a portrait of a figure from Yeats's past, the celebrated musician and clown Johnny Patterson. Born in Co. Clare in 1840, Patterson joined John Swallows's circus after buying his way out of the army. He toured Ireland and soon became well known for his solo performances, in which he sang and told jokes, and was billed as 'The Irish Singing Clown'.

Patterson discarded the traditional clown costume, replacing it with his own tweed outfit embroidered with shamrocks and a Celtic harp. He also wore a cone-shaped hat that Yeats has faithfully depicted. A national success, Patterson took up the offer of joining a circus in America in 1876 and became one of the highest paid entertainers of the time. By about 1885 he had become tired of life in America and returned to Ireland and formed his own circus. In reaction to the political situation in Ireland at the time he composed a song called *Do Your Best for One Another* in which he urged Loyalists and Nationalists to put their differences aside. During a performance of the song in 1889 rising anger in the audience resulted in a scuffle. Patterson received a blow to the head with an iron bar and three days later died in hospital.

In the painting Patterson is shown mid performance. Wearing his tweed costume he is surrounded by a group of children who sing with him under the Big Top. Other figures can be seen in the background sitting on the trestle seats or standing at the entrance. The painting is based on a watercolour sketch, since lost, that Yeats made of Patterson in 1899 from his memories of seeing the clown perform as a boy in Sligo.[1] However, while the image is rooted in an identifiable experience, in the liberal use of colour and vigorous application of paint it is also a highly expressive painting. It is the first in a series of 'great clown paintings' by Yeats in which the clown personifies man's tragic situation, both comical and courageous but yet pathetic and vulnerable.[2]

D.M.

1 Pyle 1992, I, p.343.
2 Tinney 1998, p.40.

JACK B YEATS

13

They Come, They Come, 1936

Oil on canvas, 61 x 91.5 cm
Private Collection

During the 1930s Yeats regularly revisited his earlier drawings and sketches for inspiration for his oil paintings. These works of the middle period reuse previously recorded imagery but transform it through the artist's memory, appropriating it to more mature stylistic and thematic concerns.

In *They Come, They Come* Yeats returns to an image that he made in 1919 for the illustrated periodical *Root and Branch* called *The Circus* (or *The Entry of the Clowns*). The pen and ink drawing depicts a troupe of clowns entering the circus ring at the beginning of a performance before a packed audience. One clown stares directly out of the drawing, bringing the viewer into the world of the picture.

In the oil, Yeats replicates the composition of the drawing, though in reverse, in a blaze of expressionistic colour and vigorous brushwork that reflects his interest in European Expressionism, particularly the work of Oskar Kokoschka. In contrast to the figures in the ink drawing the clowns in the oil are depicted as a far more surreal and fantastic collection of beings, epitomizing the true spirit of performance and spectacle.

From beneath a starry sky they enter the colourful tent through a red and white curtain. An elf-like creature leads the way followed by a white-faced clown, who holds his body in a contorted shape. Behind are a fiery-haired being and a snake-charmer. In the background a horse is visible alongside what appear to be other performing animals, perhaps a bear and a monkey. The horse, a favourite animal of Yeats's, was often used as a symbol of freedom. Here, although the animal is under the authority of the circus, it strides elegantly into the frame of the picture and, painted in loose brushwork, possesses an almost dreamlike quality.

D.M.

14

This Grand Conversation was under the Rose, 1943

Oil on canvas, 36 x 53 cm
NGI 4576

The title of this painting is taken from an Irish political ballad of the Napoleonic period, *The Grand Conversation under the Rose*, which Yeats illustrated in *A Broadsheet* in August 1903. The subject of the oil painting, however, has no connection with the lyrics of the ballad. Instead Yeats has adapted the title, with a touch of irony, for an image of a seemingly mundane meeting between two circus performers backstage.

It is one of a few paintings by Yeats that depicts circus performers in character and costume but removed from the usual context of their performance. The clown, the comic-buffoon, sits on a crate to rest his feet between acts, quietly drinking his cup of tea while the haute école rider, the object of his affection in the ring, leans against her horse gazing at the rose that hangs from her riding whip. Their quiet moment 'off stage' fractures the illusion of performance, exposing their true identity as fellow actors.

However there is also a more personal meaning to the painting. The rose was an important symbol for Yeats, its beauty standing as a metaphor for the solitude of the creative soul. Indeed, he painted with one pinned to his easel.[1] Yeats believed strongly that an artist should never be expected to reveal the true meaning of a work of art and regarded the rose as his personal inspiration, stating that his work was created *sub rosa*.[2] The rose appeared in paintings throughout his career and here it hangs defiantly, above the two circus performers. Under the rose the haute école rider, beautiful and elegant, becomes the artist's muse while the clown, the circus figure with whom Yeats identified most, is the reclusive artist. Their silent communication is the moment of creation, the grand conversation – *sub rosa.*

D.M.

1 Snoddy 1991, p.13.
2 For a fuller description of the events leading to Yeats's choice of the rose see Pyle 1997, p.248.

15

Alone, 1944

Oil on canvas, 46 x 61 cm
Dr. Michael Smurfit Collection

In an interval between performances a clown in full costume and make-up stands in an empty circus tent. He gazes down at his hands which appear to hold an object, perhaps a photograph or some personal momentum. His posture and sombre demeanour are similar to those of the clown in *This Grand Conversation was under the Rose* (cat. 14). Both works focus on the performer in a moment of relaxation.

The isolation of the clown is highlighted by the empty ringside seats to his left and by the opening of the tent visible above his right shoulder, through which daylight and the figures of horses and people can be seen. The triangular shape of this opening is immediately reminiscent of a spotlight which, of course, is not now on the clown.

The meaning of the work is ambiguous. The title, *Alone*, and the pensive expression of the clown suggest that it is a melancholy interpretation of the private world of the showman. However the clown could equally be construed as enjoying a moment of solitude and private thought. For an artist like Yeats, and for the circus performer, such moments of calm reflection were vital. In this context the empty tent, with its vacant seating and abandoned props is akin to a painter's studio prior to the start of work.

Yeats uses thick impasto in the depiction of the clown while in contrast the interior of the tent is sketched out in lines of colour. These are painted on an almost completely bare canvas. Yeats uses the canvas of the painting literally to represent the canvas of the circus tent. The roughly delineated forms suggest the tenuous nature of the creative act which hinges on the imagination of the artist.

R.K.

16

The Entertainers, 1945

Oil on canvas, 61 x 91.5 cm
Private Collection, courtesy Karen Reihill

A group of itinerant players are shown travelling across an open expanse of countryside. The trio is led by the dramatic figure of a man in a hat bowling a hoop. Behind him a woman in a bright yellow shawl and high heeled shoes holds an object, perhaps a sheaf of ballad songs, in her hands. The last, a man whose head is thrown back, with his face contorted in song, carries a fiddle in one hand and an enormous golden scissors in the other. The entertainers represent the three fates who in classical mythology were believed to determine man's destiny. They are usually presented as spinning the thread of life, measuring and cutting off an allotted length. These actions approximate those of the three entertainers in the painting.

Dwellings are visible in the background and bystanders have come out to look at the sudden strange appearance of the entertainers. One figure joins in their music in a frenzied dance while behind them to the left the tall figure of a woman in ragged clothing stands transfixed by their antics. Her morbid features and emaciated form are immediately reminiscent of images of the Famine. She may represent the figure of death who was often included in images of the three fates. In the bottom right hand corner the profile of a man looking up at the scene completes the circle of spectators.

The work was shown at the RHA at the end of the war in 1945. It received mixed reviews, partly because it did not subscribe to the usual euphoric mood to be found in Yeats's paintings of that period. One critic, however, did describe it as 'one of the most exciting pictures that he [Yeats] has ever shown at the academy'.[1]

The deployment of black, particularly in the sky and in the background of the painting, lends the work an ominous tone. The dilapidated dwellings and the ragged appearance of the figures resonate with the desolation of Europe at the end of the war. In this painting the entertainers signify something much more sinister than those found in Yeats's other depictions of such subjects.

R.K.

1 Goodman 1945.

17

Let 'em go and Take Care of Yourselves, 1948

Oil on canvas, 61 x 91.5 cm
Private Collection, U.K.

Let 'em go and Take Care of Yourselves is a dramatic image in which Yeats indulges in two of his great passions, horses and the circus. Rendered in thick impasto and rich, vibrant colours it is a fine example of the artist's mature style, showing him at his most theatrical and lyrical but yet personal and sentimental.

Although Yeats was generally averse to revealing the true meaning of his paintings he enjoyed the variety of explanations put forward by critics and the public. Due to the highly expressive and esoteric nature of this painting it has been the subject of various interpretations. Hilary Pyle has opined that the image is a 'late version of the circus procession', which featured in early works including *The Circus Wagon*, 1912, (see cat. 9). The blue figure to the right drives the circus wagon that bursts from the red tent and, drawn by four horses, races into the night.[1] Another interpretation suggests that the image depicts a performance at a country circus during which a team of four horses has bolted out of control. The flaps of the tent have been pulled wide to allow the horses to escape into the surrounding field. The title of the painting refers to the calls of the figure on the left to the circus hands who take his advice and leap from the path of the horses.[2]

However in his later work, Yeats infused his circus imagery with metaphor and symbolism as a method of visualizing more personal themes. In 1947, immediately following the death of his wife Cottie, he painted *The Great Tent has Collapsed* (Private Collection) as a powerful and personal expression of the grief and loss felt in the aftermath of her death. *Let 'em go and Take Care of Yourselves* may be based on a sketch produced by Yeats around the time of Cottie's death that bears the inscription *Let her go*. As the circus wagon bolts from the tent drawn by four horses towards a clear horizon, there is a distinct sense of renewal and acceptance. As the title suggests, it is a time when one must let go of grief and despair to take care of one's own existence.

D.M.

1 Pyle 1992, II, p.855.
2 Sotheby's, 1999, p.116.

18

The Last Dawn but One, 1948

Oil on canvas, 51 x 69 cm
NGI 1906

In the cold light of dawn figures are busy taking down and packing up a circus, ready to move onto their next destination. A golden-haired child stands on a dismantled Ferris wheel. Next to him in the middle distance is a figure on horseback. Yeats sketches out the forms in thick yellow, blue and red paint. In contrast, the barely painted canvas ground on which they are placed is clearly visible through the faint green of the landscape. In places Yeats has used the end of the brush to scrape into the impasto to reveal the ground underneath. The morning light illuminates the right-hand side of the scene while the night sky is still evident in the dark blues, blacks and red in the upper left hand corner.

The title, *The Last Dawn but One*, sounds almost biblical and it relates to other paintings by Yeats of the period in which he makes reference to mortality and death. Yeats, now in his seventies, had lost his wife of over 50 years the year before this work was painted. The painting refers to the ongoing routine of life. The endless task of setting up and taking down the circus is a metaphor for humanity's continual struggle to survive.

Yeats does not dwell on any of the literal details of circus life. Instead he presents the scene as a much more universal vision of human endeavour. The expanse of the landscape and the deep turquoise pool in the lower left corner, surrounded by yellow flowers, lend the scene a further biblical association. The Edenic setting stresses man's symbiotic relationship to nature, rather like that of the children of Israel whose journey through the wilderness was marked by the constant protection and goodness of their creator.

R.K.

19

The Cavalier's Farewell to his Steed, 1949

Oil on board, 36 x 46 cm
NGI 1374

The title of this painting pays homage to a famous poem by Caroline Norton, *The Arab's Farewell to his Steed*, which Yeats used as the basis for one of his most famous late horse paintings, *My Beautiful, My Beautiful* (1953, Private Collection).[1]

One can make out the striding figure of a man who turns to gaze back at his horse, his left hand raised in a gesture of farewell. The large white steed has a strange polka dot coat and no legs and is evidently a merry-go-round horse or hobby-horse of the type that Yeats saw in spectaculars in London as a young man, (see cat. 2). Clearly the painting is intended to make a humorous reference to the fantasy of the fairground or circus entertainment which allows its participants to indulge in their inner desires. Yeats emphasises the artificiality of such environments through the juxtaposition of the swaggering theatrical figure of the man and his equally outrageous prop, the hobby-horse. Central to the meaning of the work is the fact that the man is moving on from his fantasy and abandoning his toy.

Yeats's physical creation of the scene makes it all the more intriguing. As in other late works, he juxtaposes areas of thick impasto with practically bare patches of ground. Through unorthodox techniques such as the use of fingertips and brush handles, Yeats has moulded the paint to create an intricate surface. He rejects the conventional academic method of subtly building up areas of light and shade. Yet the viewer is provided with the necessary clues to make sense of the scene and to identify the light source, coming in from the right hand side. Lighting is hugely important to Yeats, both as a theatrical device and for its symbolic value as a bringer of hope and renewed aspirations. The hobby-horse stands in a darkened space indicated by the use of deep, opaque blues while the cavalier strides out into golden sunshine.

R.K.

1 Pyle 1997, p.262.

20

They Love Me, 1950

Oil on board, 35.5 x 46 cm
Private Collection, courtesy Karen Reihill

In this detail of the head and shoulders of a clown performing in a circus ring, Yeats returns to a favourite theme, (see cat. 12). To his left the audience look on, one woman stands up and cheers the performance, clearly overawed by the experience. The clown has reached the end of his act and his face betrays his inner emotions, a mixture of elation and exhaustion. The title, *They Love Me,* expresses the symbiotic relationship between the performer and the spectator. The dynamic created between these elements is central to the success of the show.

The event takes place in the interior of the circus tent. Yeats unites clown and audience through the use of a warm pinkish tone which evokes the warm darkened interior of the auditorium. It is also suggestive of the strong emotional connection made between the clown and the public as depicted in this work. The figure of the clown is built up in thick impasto, his heavily made up face and neck appear to be sculpted out of paint. The spectators, by contrast, are much more loosely sketched out in dark blue and black tones.

R.K.

JACK
B YEATS

21

Dress Rehearsal, 1951

Oil on canvas, 46 x 61 cm
Sean Galvin Collection

This late work is representative of Yeats's wider interest in the theatre and in performance in general, a theme to which the circus and travelling fair paintings closely relate. It shows a barren interior space in which a theatrical scene is being enacted. A small golden-haired child holds the reins of a large white stallion. A man dressed in a formal, almost militaristic, costume, holding a sword in one hand, kneels before them. The golden-haired child appears in other works by Yeats, (see cat. 18), and most notably in two National Gallery of Ireland paintings, *Above the Fair* (1946, NGI 1147), and *Grief* (1951, NGI 1769). The image of an armed and well-attired male figure paying homage to a raggedly dressed boy has clear religious undertones, and is reminiscent of an adoration of the magi scene in particular. This is added to by the Spartan surroundings in which the event takes place. The golden child was a symbol of hope and redemption in Yeats's work and obviously derives from the iconography of the Christ child.

Yeats was conscious of the important role of theatrical enactments and masquerades in the social life of the Irish people in the 19th and 20th centuries. His prominent inclusion of spectators in the work opens up the potential meaning of the scene to take account of its wider cultural significance. It is, as the title indicates, a dress rehearsal and thus non-performers have an active role in the drama. The foreground is dominated by three onlookers, only one of whom is actually looking at the performance. A woman whispers to her companion, while on the right-hand side another woman has turned round in her seat. She looks back out of the painting, thereby opening up the composition to allow the viewer to complete the circle and to participate in the drama.

R.K.

22

The Circus has Come, 1952

Oil on canvas, 61 x 91.5 cm
Private Collection, Ireland

A figure stands alone on a headland, silhouetted against an expanse of sea and sky. She looks down to where a circus is being erected at the edge of the shore. The painting is not concerned with the minutiae of this occurrence. Instead Yeats uses the idea of the circus metaphorically to refer to the imaginative life of the individual, represented here by the isolated onlooker.

The title, *The Circus has Come*, suggests the arrival of a significant event. Verbs concerned with movement such as coming and going, arriving and departing are found widely in the titles of Yeats's paintings. They indicate the transitory nature of emotional and psychological states of mind. The temporary nature of the circus is ideally suited to this type of theme.

Landscape plays a major role in the painting. Its expansive, untamed nature relates directly to the inner imaginative world of the figure shown within it. The boundaries between nature and the human presence appear imprecise. The vast horizon line which severs the composition just above the head of the figure can also be related to the metaphor of the circus. Both represent the world of possibilities and indicate the boundless limits of the human imagination.

R.K.

Chronology of the life of Jack B. Yeats

1871 Born youngest child of John Butler Yeats and Susan Pollexfen, London.

1879 -86 Lives with his grandparents, William and Elizabeth Pollexfen in Sligo.

1887 Joins his family in Earl's Court, London. Attends various art schools including the South Kensington School of Art, Chiswick School of Art and Westminster School of Art.

1888 Begins work as an illustrator for the *Vegetarian*. Later contributes to *Ariel* and *Paddock Life*.

1892 Poster designer for David Allen & Sons, Manchester.

1893 Staff artist on *Lika Joka*. Marries Cottie White and moves to Chertsey, Surrey.

1897 Moves to Strete, Devon. First one-man exhibition of watercolours and sketches at the Clifford Gallery, London.

1898 Visits Venice. Visits the west of Ireland and witnesses the centenary celebrations of the 1798 rebellion in Sligo.

1899 Exhibition *Sketches of Life in the West of Ireland* held at Walker Art Gallery, London and Leinster Hall, Dublin. Exhibitions of same title held almost every year until 1906. Visits World Fair, Paris.

1900 Death of his mother, Susan Pollexfen.

1902 Yeats's father and sisters, Lily and Lollie, settle in Dublin. His sisters are involved in the foundation of the Dun Emer Industries.

1904 Visits New York, exhibits at Clausen Galleries.

1905 -14 Six separate exhibitions of *Pictures of Life in the West of Ireland* held in Dublin and London.

1905 Tours west of Ireland with John M. Synge and illustrates Synge's articles for the *Manchester Guardian*.

1906 Illustrates J.M. Synge's *The Aran Islands*.

1908 His father, John Butler Yeats, moves permanently to the United States. Lily and Lollie Yeats found the Cuala Industries and the Cuala Press publishes *A Broadside* until 1915.

1910 Moves to Greystones, Co. Wicklow. Now painting mainly in oil. Begins contributing cartoons to *Punch* under the pseudonym, W. Bird.

1912 Publishes *Life in the West of Ireland*.

1913 Six works exhibited in the Armory Show in New York.

1915 Elected member of Royal Hibernian Academy.

1917 Moves to Donnybrook, closer to the centre of Dublin.

1922 Contributes to the *Exposition d'Art Irlandais* in Paris. Lectures at Irish Race Congress. Death of his father in America.

1929 Moves to Fitzwilliam Square, Dublin.

1930 Publishes first novel, *Sligo*. Meets Samuel Beckett. *The Liffey Swim* is presented to the National Gallery of Ireland by the Haverty Trust.

1933 Publishes novel, *Sailing, Sailing Swiftly*, and a trilogy of plays, *Apparitions*.

1936 Publishes novel, *The Amaranthers*.

1939 Death of his brother, W.B. Yeats.

1940 Death of his sister, Lollie Yeats.

1942 Joint exhibition with William Nicholson at the National Gallery, London. Play *La La Noo* produced by the Abbey Theatre.

1944 Publishes novel, *And to You Also*.

1945 *Jack B. Yeats. National Loan Exhibition* held in Dublin. Thomas MacGreevy's monograph, *Jack B. Yeats. An Appreciation and an Interpretation*, published. First exhibition at Victor Waddington Galleries.

1947 Death of his wife, Cottie.

1948 Solo exhibition at Tate Gallery, London.

1949 Play *In Sand* produced by the Abbey Theatre. Death of his sister, Lily Yeats.

1954 Exhibition at Galerie Beaux-Arts, Paris.

1955 Moves permanently into a nursing home at Portobello House.

1957 Dies on 28 March.

Bibliography

Arnold 1998
Bruce Arnold, *Jack Yeats*, (New Haven & London, 1998).

Croft-Cooke & Cotes 1976
Rupert Croft-Cooke & Peter Cotes, *Circus: A World History*, (London, 1976).

Goodman 1945
Theodore Goodman, 'At the Royal Hibernian Academy', *Commentary*, May 1945, p.13.

Potterton 1993
Homan Potterton, 'Jack B. Yeats and John Quinn', *Irish Arts Review*, 1993, pp.102-14.

Purser 1991
John W. Purser, *The Literary Works of Jack B. Yeats*, (Gerrards Cross, 1991).

Pyle 1970
Hilary Pyle, *Jack B. Yeats. A Biography*, (London, 1970).

Pyle 1992
Hilary Pyle, *Jack B. Yeats. A Catalogue Raisonné of the Oil Paintings,* 3 vols, (London, 1992).

Pyle 1993
Hilary Pyle, *Jack B. Yeats: His Watercolours, Drawings and Pastels,* (Dublin, 1993).

Pyle 1994
Hilary Pyle, *The Different Worlds of Jack B. Yeats. His Cartoons and Illustrations*, (Dublin, 1994)

Pyle 1997
Hilary Pyle, *Yeats. Portrait of an Artistic Family*, (Dublin, 1997).

Rooney 2006
Brendan Rooney et al, *A Time and A Place. Two Centuries of Irish Social Life,* (Dublin, 2006).

Rosenthal 1993
T. G. Rosenthal, *The Art of Jack B. Yeats*, (London, 1993).

Snoddy 1991
Stephen Snoddy et al, *Jack B. Yeats. The Late Paintings*, (Bristol, London, The Hague, 1991).

Sotheby's 1999
The Irish Sale, Sotheby's London, 21 May 1999.

Speaight 1980
George Speaight, *A History of the Circus,* (London, 1980).

Stoddart 2000
Helen Stoddart, *Rings of Desire. Circus History and Representation,* (Manchester, 2000).

Synge 1911
John M. Synge, *In Wicklow, West Kerry and Connemara,* (Dublin, 1911).

Tinney 1998
Donal Tinney, ed., *Jack B. Yeats at the Niland Gallery Sligo,* (Sligo, 1998).

Yeats 1912
Jack B. Yeats, *Life in the West of Ireland*, (Dublin, 1912).

Photo Credits

Figs 1-3, 5, 7-11 © Estate of Jack B. Yeats/DACS London, 2007
Images © The National Gallery of Ireland, Photographer: Roy Hewson

Fig. 4 Image © National Gallery London

Fig. 6 © Succession Picasso/DACS London 2007
Digital Image © 2007, The Museum of Modern Art, NY/Scala, Florence

Cats 1, 2, 4, 5, 9, 10, 12, 14, 16, 18-21 © Estate of Jack B. Yeats/DACS London. 2007
Images © The National Gallery of Ireland, Photographer: Roy Hewson

Cats 3, 7 © Estate of Jack B. Yeats/DACS, London 2007
Photo courtesy of Dublin City Gallery, The Hugh Lane
Photographer John Kellett

Cats 6, 13, 22 © Estate of Jack B. Yeats/DACS London, 2007

Cat. 8 © Estate of Jack B. Yeats/DACS London, 2007
Photo © Waddington Galleries

Cat. 11 © Estate of Jack B. Yeats/DACS London, 2007
Photo© Studioworks Photography

Cats 15, 17 © Estate of Jack B. Yeats/DACS London, 2007
Photo © Christies Images Ltd, 2007

Published in conjunction with the exhibition *Masquerade and Spectacle: The Circus and the Travelling Fair in the work of Jack B. Yeats* at the National Gallery of Ireland 18 July–11 November 2007

Distribution worldwide by the National Gallery of Ireland

ISBN 978-1-904288-24-4

Edited by Dr. Róisín Kennedy

Catalogue entries:
Dr. Róisín Kennedy
Donal Maguire
Iain Wynn-Jones

Catalogue designed by Jason Ellams
Printed in Dublin by Colorman Ireland Ltd

Cover Image: Jack B. Yeats, *Double Jockey Act*, 1916.
Oil on canvas, 61 x 46 cm. NGI 1737 (cat. 10)

In association with:

PIONEER Investments®